SONGS OF THE SEASON

Study by Mark Wingfield
Commentary by Judson Edwards

Free downloadable Teaching Guide for this study available at
NextSunday.com/teachingguides

NextSunday Resources
6316 Peake Road
Macon, Georgia 31210-3960
1-800-747-3016
©2019 by NextSunday Resources
All rights reserved.

TABLE OF CONTENTS

Songs of the Season

HOW TO USE THIS STUDY

NextSunday Resources Adult Bible Studies are designed to help adults study Scripture seriously within the context of the larger Christian tradition and, through that process, find their faith renewed, challenged, and strengthened. We study the Scriptures because we believe they affect our current lives in important ways. Each study contains the following three components:

Study Guide

Each study guide lesson is arranged in four movements:

Reflecting recalls a contemporary story, anecdote, example, or illustration to help us anticipate the session's relevance in our lives.

Studying is centered on giving the biblical material in-depth attention while often surrounding it with helpful insights from theology, ethics, church history, and other areas.

Understanding helps us find relevant connections between our lives and the biblical message.

What About Me? provides brief statements that help unite life issues with the meaning of the biblical text.

Commentary

Each study guide lesson is accompanied by an additional, in-depth commentary on the biblical material. Written by a different author than the study guide, each commentary gives the opportunity for learners to approach the Scripture text from a separate but complementary viewpoint.

Teaching Guide

In addition to the provided study guide and commentary, *NextSunday Resources* also provides a *free* downloadable teaching guide, available at NextSunday.com. Each teaching guide gives the teacher tools for focusing on the content of each study guide lesson through additional commentary and Bible background information. Through teacher helps and teaching options, each teaching guide also provides substance for variety and choice in the preparation of each lesson.

NextSunday
Resources

STUDY INTRODUCTION

One of the most dearly beloved aspects of the Christmas season is the music. From songs on the radio to church cantatas to school holiday concerts, Christmas means music. Some of this music is secular, but who doesn't start tapping their toes to "Winter Wonderland"? For Christians, the most precious songs of the season are those that celebrate the coming of Christ, born as a baby in the little town of Bethlehem.

Before any of our Christmas favorites were composed, people of faith celebrated the newborn King through song. In this study, we will explore some of the songs of the season recorded for us in Scripture.

We'll begin with one of the so-called "Servant Songs" of Isaiah as we contemplate the mission of Jesus—and us!—to be a light to the nations. Then we'll study the four songs found in the first two chapters of Luke and listen as Mary, Zechariah, the angels, and finally Simeon guide us in praising, proclaiming, and interpreting the meaning of Christ's coming.

THE SERVANT'S SONG

Isaiah 49:1-6

Central Question

How can I follow Jesus in being a "light to the nations"?

Scripture

Isaiah 49:1-6 Listen to me, coastlands; pay attention, peoples far away. The LORD called me before my birth, called my name when I was in my mother's womb. 2 He made my mouth like a sharp sword, and hid me in the shadow of God's own hand. He made me a sharpened arrow, and concealed me in God's quiver, 3 saying to me, "You are my servant, Israel, in whom I show my glory." 4 But I said, "I have wearied myself in vain. I have used up my strength for nothing." Nevertheless, the LORD will grant me justice; my reward is with my God. 5 And now the LORD has decided— the one who formed me from the womb as his servant— to restore Jacob to God, so that Israel might return to him. Moreover, I'm honored in the LORD's eyes; my God has become my strength. 6 He said: It is not enough, since you are my servant, to raise up the tribes of Jacob and to bring back the survivors of Israel. Hence, I will also appoint you as light to the nations so that my salvation may reach to the end of the earth.

Reflecting

A few years ago at youth camp, our student minister unveiled a video surprise for the campers each morning. He had worked in advance with a well-known radio personality and voice-over talent in our congregation—a man with a resonant and serious voice—to record the spoken lyrics to popular songs. Here was the straight radio newsman, seated in a big stuffed chair, dryly reading aloud the lyrics, for example, to a Justin Bieber song: "Baby, baby, oh, baby, baby, baby." Stripped of a melody and souped-up studio production techniques, these pop-song lyrics were exposed for what they are: vapid drivel.

The result was hysterical. Every morning, the teenage campers eagerly awaited that day's installment of pop-lyric humor. The very songs they normally listened to on the radio took on a strange and humorous perspective when read aloud by a mature adult as though they were pages out of a novel.

When reading this lesson's Scripture, we may feel a similar sensation and wonder how on earth these words ever could be construed as a "song." What's the tune? Where are the rhymes? Where is there a cadence? And what's the point?

? How can we best appreciate the songs of the Bible when we don't know the tune, tempo, etc.?

Huge portions of the Old Testament—some say up to seventy-five percent—were written as poetry, perhaps because it was easier to remember or to set to music, which also would help with memory. This poetry does not take the form of English ideals about poetry, although we may most closely see the connection in Psalms and Proverbs.

We English readers may have difficulty finding the poetry in the translation of ancient Hebrew texts. Sometimes, things really do get lost in translation—not only in linguistic translation, but in cultural translation. When all else fails, we at least can seek to understand the gist of the conversation. And in this case, the thesis statement jumps out from the last sentence of the poem: "I will also appoint you as light to the nations so that my salvation may reach to the end of the earth."

These words may not sound melodic to our ears, but they nonetheless form the steady beat of much of Christian theology, and especially of New Testament integration of Old Testament prophecies. From this Servant Song, we pick up a recurring motif of God's plan to reveal a light to the nations.

Studying

Is there a more controversial book in the Bible than Isaiah? Sure, Christians love to argue about Genesis and Revelation, who wrote what when, and whether the stories are literal or figurative. But if you want to get to the heart of interfaith disagreement, Isaiah is ground zero. I suspect Christians and Jews might more easily find agreement in the Gospels than in Isaiah—and particularly in the so-called Servant Songs, where we find ourselves this lesson.

Isaiah stands at the center of conservative Christians' argument against principles of academic critique applied to the Bible by less conservative folks. Was this huge book written by one author, by two, or by three? Did the prophet named Isaiah write any of it? That is an academic debate, and an interesting one. But Isaiah also takes us to the heart of what separates Jews and Christians the most: prophecies of the Messiah.

Christians have a hard time understanding why observant Jews don't acknowledge that Jesus clearly came as God's promised Messiah. I recall vividly a conversation I had years ago with a Jewish leader when he was asked why he didn't believe Jesus was the prophesied Messiah. His answer was short: "Because he doesn't fit the biblical description."

To Christians, it's perfectly clear, as we interpret the Old Testament in light of the New Testament, that Jesus is the Messiah. From our vantage point, Jesus fits the description of all the Old Testament prophecies. From a modern Jewish perspective, however, Jesus does not fit the bill.

While most Christians will read this lesson's passage from Isaiah and immediately identify the Servant mentioned here as Jesus, most Jewish scholars will disagree. In their eyes, the Servant is most likely Israel itself or a figure from Israel's past.

Our passage this lesson is the second of four Servant Songs identified as unique poetry within the book of Isaiah. The first song is found in Isaiah 42:1-4, the third song is found in Isaiah 50:4-9, and the fourth song is found in Isaiah 52:13–53:12. These are "songs" in the sense that they are written as poetry.

The Servant, sometimes referred to by Christians and Jews alike as the "Suffering Servant," is a character who receives a mandate from the Lord to "bring justice to the nations" (42:1). This Servant becomes a "bruised reed" that will not break (42:3), is "despised and avoided by others" (53:3), and bears our sufferings as his affliction (53:4).

So ubiquitous is the Christian identification of the Servant with Jesus that few Christians would take the time to understand that someone else might read these passages differently. If you believe that Jesus is, in fact, the Messiah, who was wounded for our transgressions and took upon himself the iniquity of us all (53:5), how could you not identify Jesus as the Suffering Servant?

We come to this viewpoint not on our own, but with guidance from the New Testament writers, particularly the Apostle Paul, and even Jesus himself. Recall that Jesus' public ministry began when he read aloud a portion of Isaiah 61 in the synagogue at Nazareth: *"The Spirit of the Lord is upon me, because the Lord has anointed me. He has sent me to preach good news to the poor...and to proclaim the year of the Lord's favor"* (Luke 4:18-19). This passage is highly suggestive of the work of the Servant in Isaiah's Servant Songs. Throughout the Gospels, Jesus tells his disciples that he must suffer and die on their behalf, further echoing the Suffering Servant motif.

For Paul's part, look to Romans 4:25, where he says Jesus was "handed over because of our mistakes" and "raised to meet the requirements of righteousness for us," a direct quotation from the fourth Servant Song. These ideas also are developed in Galatians 3 and 2 Corinthians 5, among other passages.

The Jewish interpretation of Isaiah's servant as a faithful remnant within Israel is not entirely wrong, however. After all, even Paul inter-prets Isaiah 49 as referring to the church in Acts 13:49. The mandate to be a "light to the nations" (Isa 49:6) belongs to God's people as much as it does God's Messiah. That is something we learned from Judaism. The tradi-tional Christian teaching goes something like this:

> This is what the Lord commanded us: *I have made you a light for the Gentiles, so that you could bring salvation to the end of the earth.* (Acts 13:47)

(1) God chose Israel to be a light to the nations, to teach the world about God.

(2) Israel rebelled against God time and again, failing to fulfill this calling.

(3) Therefore, God sent Jesus to be the faithful Israelite who completes Israel's mission of glorifying God (see Isa 49:3).

(4) Jesus the Messiah has now established the church, the messianic community, to extend God's love and care to Jew and Gentile alike.

For their part, the Jewish people believe they have been and are a light to the nations, but in a different way than Christians might associate with Isaiah's prophecy. Jews account for only 0.2 percent of the world's population but have had a disproportionately huge influence on advances in every field from medicine to science to ethics to politics to economics. Some Jewish apologists portray their tiny population as the most influential people group the world has ever known. For example, about one-fifth of all recipients of the Nobel Prize have been Jewish. By giving leadership to the advancement of society, the Jewish people believe they are driven to be a light to the nations.

> Concern with foreign nations is a recurring theme in Isaiah; see Isaiah 2:2-4; 11:10; 19:19-25; 25:6-9; 42:1-4; 52:15; 56:3-7; 60:3; 61:9; 62:10; 66:18-19, 23. The theme of God's salvation reaching earth's ends is consistent with the portrayal of God as the world's sole creator. **1175 OT**

The key for Christian interpretation of Isaiah 49:6, however, is in the combined clauses of the last sentence: "I will also appoint you as light to the nations *so that my salvation may reach to the end of the earth*" (emphasis mine). Christians see in the Servant's mandate a story of salvation, not merely of social advancement.

Understanding

On this first Sunday of Advent, we might connect Isaiah's Servant with the declaration of another popular Advent text from Isaiah 60:1, "Arise! Shine! Your light has come; the LORD's glory has shone upon you."

The entirety of this lesson's passage illustrates God's desire for restoration with those who are estranged from God. This restoration happens not because of what we do ourselves but because of what God offers us.

The same is true of the light that shines. Nowhere in Isaiah's prophecy is the Servant said to be the source of the light, just as we are not the source of God's light. "I will also appoint you as light," God tells the Servant (49:6). This is matched by the later expression in Isaiah 60:1 that "*the LORD's glory* has shone upon you" (emphasis mine).

We may think of this light-emitting mission as similar to the work of a lighthouse on a rocky shore. Lighthouses serve as beacons to guide ships into port or to keep them away from hazards in the water. They do this not simply by emitting light but by reflecting and magnifying light. The modern lighthouse lamp was invented in 1822 by Augustine Fresnel, who created a means of crafting glass into a beehive shape that projects the source light up to twenty miles. This invention was so revolutionary that lighthouses thereafter had to be built taller in order for the increased range to overcome the curvature of the earth.

When we think of our individual, family, or congregational witness as a bringer of light for God, it is important to remember that we are not the light. Instead, we reflect God's light. When we magnify the Lord (see Ps 34:3), we spread life-giving light far away. And when we stand up tall, figuratively speaking, we shine the light even farther.

What About Me?

• *When have you listened to the faith perspectives of Jewish neighbors, relatives, or friends?* Although this is a sensitive topic, there are ways to engage in meaningful and cordial dialogue. Consider finding a way during this Advent season to hear and understand the faith perspective of another.

• *Who do you think the Servant of Isaiah is meant to be?* How you answer this question could shape the way you read much of the rest of the Bible. Remember that the best practice for Christian theology is to read the Old Testament in light of the New Testament—but not to twist Old Testament passages to serve New Testament ideas.

• *How are we to read the messianic prophecies of the Old Testament?* There are numerous other texts in Isaiah that are often read during this season (Isa 7, 9, and 40, in particular). How can we read these passages responsibly, giving full weight to their original historical context before examining how they have been received in Christian tradition?

• *How do you identify with the Servant of Isaiah 49?* Are there particular words or phrases in this poetry that jump out at you or offer unique insight? Read the passage again and imagine that this is God's direction to you. Does that change the meaning in any way?

• *What does it mean to be a "light to the nations"?* How might this imagery connect with Jesus' declaration that his followers are "the salt of the earth" and "the light of the world" (Matt 5:13-14)?

• *How can you reflect the light of God?* Is it possible that your own light outshines God's to those around you? What are ways that you might magnify the Lord as a lighthouse magnifies light to the watching ships?

THE SERVANT'S SONG

Isaiah 49:1-6

Introduction

Christmas just wouldn't be Christmas without music. Can you imagine the Advent season without "Joy to the World," "Hark, the Herald Angels Sing," and "Away in a Manger"? Can you fathom a Christmas Eve service without candles and "Silent Night"? No, Christmas without the songs of Christmas wouldn't be Christmas at all.

This Advent season, we're going to study some of the songs of Christmas in the Bible. Our first study focuses on one of the Servant Songs in the book of Isaiah. There are four Servant Songs (Isa 42:1-4, 49:1-6, 50:4-9, and 52:13–53:12), and they all deal with a mysterious, unnamed servant who would do remarkable things for Israel.

The identity of the servant in these songs is confusing. In some of the songs, it seems that the nation of Israel itself is the servant. At times, the prophet Isaiah seems to be the servant. For centuries, the Christian community has identified Jesus as the unnamed servant in these songs.

I suppose it doesn't really matter who this servant was. In her book *Gospel Medicine* (Boston: Cowley, 1995), Barbara Brown Taylor writes,

> In the end, it does not matter whether we can name the person Isaiah paints for us, because the portrait already has a name. "God's Servant," it says, and that is enough. This is God's Chosen One, and whether the words are capitalized or not they speak to all of us who are God's servants in this world. Whether we like it or not, every one of us is a full-fledged deputy of God's kingdom. Some of us are better at it than others and some of us

do more harm than good, but none of us is excused. The moment we were baptized as Christ's own forever, we were set apart as God's servants in this world, and the very fact that we are still hanging around means that we have not resigned yet. (159)

That's another way to come at this servant song in Isaiah 49. We can see this passage as describing our own experience as the servant of God and telling us what we need to do to be a light to others. Certainly, we can see this first Christmas song as a messianic prophecy, describing the life and ministry of Jesus. But we can also see it as describing *our* life and ministry as one of Jesus' followers.

Great Expectations

Our song begins with high hopes and great expectations. The servant announces that God called him before his birth, called his name when he was in his mother's womb. The Lord also made his mouth sharp like a sword and hid him in the shadow of God's own hand. God even announced to him that he was God's servant in whom God would reveal his glory. With resources like that working for him, how could the servant fail?

I would guess that most of us who see ourselves as servants of God would declare those same truths about our relationship with God. As servants of God, we believe that we are:

• *Called.* It's not as if we finally received enough information and courage to choose God. No, we believe that God, amazingly, has chosen us. Our relationship with God is more God's doing than ours. For reasons we can't quite articulate, God called us before we were born and named us when we were in our mother's womb. God has called us, and we spend our days trying to be faithful to that call.

• *Inspired.* Like the servant in our verses, we sense that God has made our mouth sharp like a sword. God has inspired us to declare things that have made a surprising difference to others. We have been able to write, sing, preach, comfort, and cajole because God has made our mouth sharp like a sword. At times, we look back on something we have said, written, or sung and sensed that our words were not our own.

• *Comforted.* We also know what it's like to rest in the shadow of God's hand. In our times of grief, confusion, depression, and failure, we have felt the hand of God on us, giving us strength and comfort. We sometimes find ourselves whispering with the Apostle Paul, "I can endure all these things through the power of the one who gives me strength" (Phil 4:13).

• *Used.* Incredibly, we can look back on certain times in our lives when God used us to show divine glory. We were able to be agents of hope, reconciliation, wisdom, or joy to others. The finest moments in our lives are those times when we are able to be the very presence and glory of God to someone else.

When the servant of God in Isaiah 49 began to sing his song, he was filled with great expectations. He knew he was called, inspired, comforted, and used by God, and his future was filled with possibility.

Unexpected Burnout

Verse 4 adds a note of somber reality. Things hadn't exactly gone as the servant had planned. His great expectations had not been realized. Instead, he had grown weary and disillusioned. He had used up his strength for nothing.

Our society has coined a word we all know about and maybe have even experienced: burnout. The word has even made it into the dictionary. Mine defines it as "emotional exhaustion from mental stress."

The chances are good that if we haven't burned ourselves out, we know someone who has. Schoolteachers are burning out. So are pastors and other church staff members. Church members sometimes burn out, as do parents. Burnout is what happens when we burn the candle at both ends until there's no candle left.

Even though burnout is a fairly new addition to the dictionary, it is obviously not a new phenomenon. Isaiah 49 is the testimony of a godly servant dealing with what most definitely sounds likes burnout. He starts out called, inspired, comforted, and used, and ends up weary, with all of his strength used up. He assumed he would be used; he had no idea he would be *used up*.

We have no statistics telling us how often that happens among Christians today, but my guess is it happens a lot. We Christians feel a lot of pressure to perform. After all, we're servants of God, which means we ought to be extraordinary. Shouldn't a servant of God be extra thoughtful, extra friendly, extra caring? Aren't we the only Bible someone might ever read?

So we volunteer, join, serve, listen, and give. We go the extra mile and always keep smiles on our faces. We're good people, but we also know we're never good enough. The goal of being a better Christian is always before us.

And then, quite by surprise, there comes the day when we feel just like this servant in Isaiah 49. We feel like we've labored in vain, that we really haven't made much of a difference to anyone. That dastardly condition known as burnout has sneaked up on us and robbed us of our joy.

Being Light

The most surprising thing about these verses is what happens next. We would assume that God would tell the servant to get his act together, try harder, recommit himself to a life of service, and then he might be useful again. When a servant of God burns out, that servant is no longer able to do much for God, right?

Wrong! The servant discovers that he is still honored in God's eyes and that he can still receive strength from God. He even discovers that God has bigger things in store for him. Not only will he minister to Judah and Israel, he will also be a light to the nations so that God's salvation may reach to the ends of the earth.

In essence, God says to the servant, "I just want you to shine, to be a light. I don't want you to be successful or busy or super-spiritual. I just want you to have some spark, to shine, to *be* something."

Barbara Brown Taylor comments on God's message to this servant and how this message applies to us today:

What if the real test of our success as God's servants is not what we do but how we do it? What if the real measure of our extraordinariness as Christians is not our thoughtfulness or our friendliness or our busyness but our *spark*? What if the real sign of our witness to the light is not how much we accomplish but our own *lightness*, our own reflection of the bright God who has chosen us and lit us up and sent us into the world like candles in a dark room? (161)

I love something Anne Lamott says in her book *Bird by Bird* (New York: Doubleday, 1994): "Lighthouses don't go running all over an island looking for boats to save; they just stand there shining" (236). That, I think, was God's message to the servant in Isaiah 49. God wanted him to just stand there shining. And that may well be God's message to us, too—especially if we're feeling burned out and disillusioned.

What if our assignment this Advent season is to quit trying to perform and just relax and *be*? What if we make it a priority to spend this Advent getting closer to the Light so that we can have more spark ourselves? What if we quit trying to do something for God and let God do something in us?

Conclusion

In coming lessons, we will hear some other songs of Christmas. Next, we'll listen to Mary's song, the *Magnificat*, in Luke 1. Then we'll listen to Zechariah's song, traditionally called the *Benedictus*, a song of praise also in Luke 1. Then we'll hear the Angels' song in Luke 2 and be reminded just how good our Good News is. Finally, we'll hear Simeon's song at the end of Luke 2, as he sings his song of joy upon first seeing the Christ child in the temple. There is definitely music in the air in the first two chapters of Luke. For the next four lessons, we'll be listening to it.

But the Servant's Song in Isaiah 49 is a perfect prelude to these other songs. It enables all of us who consider ourselves to be servants of God to do a beginning-of-Advent inventory.

We can count our blessings that God has called, inspired, comforted, and used us in spite of our sins and mistakes. We can express our gratitude that we have been called to be a servant of God.

We can ask if burnout is robbing us of our joy and evaluate how much spark we have in our lives. We can consider how discouraged and disillusioned we have become.

And we can hear God whispering to us to be light, to cease all of our spiritual activity for a while, and just try to get closer to the Source of Light. Even if we're battling burnout, we can hear God promise to bless us and use us to be a light to the nations.

There are many lessons we can learn as we hear all of these Christmas songs in the upcoming lessons. But the one lesson that seems to stand out in this first one is this: as we begin the Advent season, we should relax into the goodness of God so that we can "just stand there shining."

God, as we approach this Advent season, we would like to have more spark, to have more joy, to be more alive. But we also know that we can't produce these things by trying harder. In fact, it seems the harder we try, the more burned out we become. So we want to be still these next few weeks and know that you are God. We want to become so aware of your presence in our lives that, like Moses, our faces will shine. We pray this in the name of one who called himself "the light of the world," Jesus our Lord. Amen.

Notes

Notes

2

MARY'S SONG

Luke 1:41-55

Central Question

When have I experienced great things from God?

Scripture

Luke 1:41-55 When Elizabeth heard Mary's greeting, the child leaped in her womb, and Elizabeth was filled with the Holy Spirit. 42 With a loud voice she blurted out, "God has blessed you above all women, and he has blessed the child you carry. 43 Why do I have this honor, that the mother of my Lord should come to me? 44 As soon as I heard your greeting, the baby in my womb jumped for joy. 45 Happy is she who believed that the Lord would fulfill the promises he made to her." 46 Mary said, "With all my heart I glorify the Lord! 47 In the depths of who I am I rejoice in God my savior. 48 He has looked with favor on the low status of his servant. Look! From now on, everyone will consider me highly favored 49 because the mighty one has done great things for me. Holy is his name. 50 He shows mercy to everyone, from one generation to the next, who honors him as God. 51 He has shown strength with his arm. He has scattered those with arrogant thoughts and proud inclinations. 52 He has pulled the powerful down from their thrones and lifted up the lowly. 53 He has filled the hungry with good things and sent the rich away empty-handed. 54 He has come to the aid of his servant Israel, remembering his mercy, 55 just as he promised to our ancestors, to Abraham and to Abraham's descendants forever."

Reflecting

The closing line from last lesson's text, the call to be a "light to the nations" (Isa 49:6), did not resonate with the contemporaries of William Carey in eighteenth-century England. Carey, a young and newly ordained Baptist minister, had become convinced that Christians should be engaged in missionary work to tell the gospel story to those who had never heard it. He took seriously the call of the Servant Song to become a light to the nations.

That wasn't the prevailing view of the day, when the Calvinistic belief that Christ's atoning work was intended only for the elect was predominant. Thus, when the young Carey stood up at an associational meeting to speak of the need for international missions, so the story goes, an older minister quickly shot him down: "Young man, sit down!" he said. "You are an enthusiast. When God pleases to convert the heathen, he'll do it without consulting you or me."

In 1792, Carey organized a missionary society. At its first meeting, he preached a sermon with the theme, "Expect great things; attempt great things." This phrase is sometimes expanded to include the full sense of what Carey intended: "Expect great things from God; attempt great things for God."

When no one else would go, Carey, his family, and one friend set sail for India, where they launched the modern missionary movement. William Carey is widely considered the father of modern Christian missions. His call to expect great things and attempt great things echoes through history and has shaped who we are today as twenty-first-century Christians.

Carey's words could have been inspired by this lesson's text. The *Magnificat* of Mary, one of four canticles of Christmas recorded in Luke's Gospel, demonstrates how all things are possible with God. "The mighty one has done great things for me" (Luke 1:49), says Mary, who bears the very Son of God in human form.

Studying

A canticle is a hymn or chant drawn from a biblical text other than the Psalms.

Our text this lesson most often is known as the *Magnificat*, a title taken from the first word of the Song of Mary in the Latin translation. As with last lesson's text, these verses are called a song because they are set in a poetic form, not because they were originally set to music. To understand the placement and role of this poem, however, we might look to a traditional theatrical musical, where lines of spoken dialogue are interrupted by musical numbers that illustrate the plot development at that point.

The *Magnificat* is like that. It stands apart as a poetic expression of the facts we have been told in the narrative. The story of Luke 1 could be read without the Song of Mary and still make perfect sense. See for yourself by reading to verse 45 and immediately jumping to verse 56.

One of the problems with familiar Scripture passages (such as all those associated with Jesus' birth) is that we as readers fail to think critically about what we are reading. This story is so familiar to most Christians that we easily overlook the first question someone new to the story might ask: "Did Mary really burst into song when she met Elizabeth?"

The answer to that question is most likely no. Consider the facts: Mary likely was a girl of about thirteen with little or no formal education, living in a small village in Galilee. Even if she did have the wherewithal, guided by the Holy Spirit, to utter a perfectly phrased poem spontaneously, who had a tape recorder? How could it have been written down verbatim?

This is not to suggest that Mary did not say something like these words, either at the time or later on. That is entirely possible because the *Magnificat* echoes a portion of the Hebrew Bible called the Song of Hannah, found in 1 Samuel 2:1-10. As a devout Jew, Mary would have heard and was perhaps well acquainted with Hannah's song. It also is possible that Luke inserted this hymn or poem into his Gospel as a summary of Mary's response to Elizabeth's greeting and all the other events taking place in her life.

Either way, what we see here is one of the first New Testament hymns. It is a hymn that grants us insight into the mind of one who had the audacity to expect great things from God and allowed herself to be used to bring about great things for God.

This hymn of praise occurs in a particular context that is important to remember. Mary, having just been visited by an angel, has been told that she will become pregnant with the Messiah, the Son of God. No doubt confused, scared, and dumbfounded, she travels to visit her "relative" (v. 36), perhaps an aunt, who is also pregnant.

Mary's words are called the *Magnificat*, which is the first word in the Latin translation of this poem. Like many psalms that praise God (e.g., Ps 34, 105), and like Hannah's prayer (1 Sam 2:1-10), Mary's Song offers reasons why praise is the right response. Her song can function as either a call to praise or a prayer, even though it's not addressed directly to God. The first part (1:46-50) focuses on what God has done for Mary. The second part (1:51-55) moves on to what God has done for all, especially Israel. Mary is thinking ahead, previewing what Jesus will do by God's direction. **107 NT**

We can imagine Mary wanting to get out of town while she can. The traditional location of Elizabeth's home is in Ein Karem, eighty miles from Nazareth, where Mary lived. This journey may have taken Mary more than a week.

When Mary greeted Elizabeth, the baby in Elizabeth's womb (John the Baptist) "jumped for joy" (v. 44). This fulfilled a prophecy that an angel had spoken to Elizabeth's husband, Zechariah. This is recorded in Luke 1:15, when the angel says the baby Elizabeth will bear will be "filled with the Holy Spirit even before his birth."

Pause here to reflect upon the primacy of two female characters in this pivotal story. Although the Bible is full of patriarchs, often it is the women through whom great things happen and great things are recognized. Elizabeth's role is brief, but still she shines as a woman of faith who dares to believe in great things from God. She becomes the first prophet in Luke's Gospel.

Much has been speculated about how much Mary may have understood about what was happening to her. A casual reading of this canticle of Mary might lead one to believe that, after the angelic visitation, she had it all figured out instantly and could

speak cogently about deep theological truths. The power of the Holy Spirit notwithstanding, it again seems more likely that this song of praise reflects a later and more neatly organized reflection upon what Mary experienced on that day and in the days ahead.

Are we meant to find comfort in the Song of Mary? Parts of it may well be comforting, but other aspects can be frightening. Yes, it is a song of praise to God. But most of us are not prepared for the reasons Mary gives to praise God. Read these verses carefully and perhaps even write down what Mary is thankful for. We're on board with God showing "mercy to everyone" (v. 50) because we're included in "everyone." Don't forget, though, that "everyone" includes even those people we don't like and don't think deserve any mercy. And what about God scattering the arrogant, pulling down the powerful, filling the hungry, and sending the rich away empty-handed (vv. 51-53)? Are we prepared to praise God for that?

Christians in America may easily overlook the radical social nature of the *Magnificat*—which is echoed in Jesus' teachings and part of what got him in trouble with the establishment. Jesus taught a reversal of roles, that the first would be last and the rich would be made poor (see Luke 6:24-25). The coming of Jesus, foreshadowed here by Mary's song, ushers in not only an elevation of those who are lowly, but also a knocking down of those who are exalted.

Before we jump on the bandwagon to gleefully sing Mary's song, we have to face up to which side of the status quo we currently live on. We hear these same ideas summarized in James 4:10—"Humble yourselves before the Lord, and he will lift you up."

Likewise, Mary challenges us to reconsider one of the most overused words of American Christianity: "blessed." Many English translations use this word in the second phrase of verse 48: "All generations shall call me blessed" (NRSV). We most often use this word to describe material success, but Mary uses it to describe being in line with God's purpose for her life. That's similar to what Jesus later would do in the Beatitudes, when he said, "Blessed are you..." (Matt 5:3-11; Luke 6:20-22, NRSV). The next time you hear yourself say, "I'm so blessed," stop and ask how your definition of "blessed" compares to Mary's.

Understanding

As I write, I have just returned from our church's annual youth camp. Our theme was "Get Out the Map." Through several biblical stories, we talked about the road of life and how sometimes unpredictable the journey map be—so unpredictable that we can't usually map out even a five-year plan of our own making. The map, we learned at camp, is more about being than about doing. It's more about knowing how to find your way than following turn-by-turn directions. As with using GPS to find a destination, you can dutifully follow instructions and still not understand how you arrived at the right place.

We wanted the youth to understand that the kind of person you are is more important than what you do for a living. "What kind of job do you want when you grow up?" is not the best question. "What kind of person do you want to be with God's help?" is a better question.

What we learn from Mary is that faithful obedience to God's nudging matters most. Even when we want to attempt great things for God, we may not be able to chart ahead what those great things are—and if we try, we're likely to be wrong. More often, the great things we do for God happen when opportunity knocks, in the spur of the moment, or when we set aside our careful plans and follow the guidance of the Holy Spirit.

How tightly are you holding on to your map for life? Could you let go and follow the guidance of an angelic visitation if one came to you? Like Mary, William Carey knew that attempting great things for God had to be paired with expecting great things from God—not for our own benefit but for the sake of God's purposes.

> Do you expect "great things" (v. 49) from God? Why or why not? (And what is your definition of "great"?)

What About Me?

• *Christmas is a season of giving—and of expecting to receive.* It's hard to be honest about our own expectations and anticipations in this season. In the same way, it is hard to read our favorite Christmas passages with open minds. Find a way to reread Mary's story in a fresh way, either using a different translation or by reading more carefully. Ask the Holy Spirit to speak God's truth to you in new ways as you seek to be open to something new and different.

• *What has God uniquely equipped you to do for good in the world?* Sometimes, the great things we can do are right in front of us and come naturally, if only we will recognize them. If you have been given the gift of succeeding in business, to what end might God have enriched your life? If you have the gift of hospitality, are you ever hospitable with anyone outside your current circle of friends? Imagine yourself as a teenager once again and rather than asking what you want to be when you grow up or what your major should be in college, ask yourself what kind of person you want to be. Have you become, or are you becoming, that kind of person?

• *What great things has God done in your life?* A few days ago, I had lunch with a friend who is a recovering alcoholic and drug addict. In sobriety, he has known great success as a businessman and has offered himself to help many others find their way out of the ditch. Even so, he sometimes replays the old tapes about how bad things are, how difficult life is, how frustrating everything appears. When that happens, he said, he has trained himself to create a gratitude list. He stops what he's doing and forces himself to list the true blessings he has known. As soon as he does that, his outlook takes a 180-degree turn. Gratitude is a gift that keeps on giving.

Resource

Richard B. Vinson, *Luke*, Smyth & Helwys Bible Commentary (Macon GA: Smyth & Helwys, 2008).

MARY'S
SONG

Luke 1:41-55

Introduction

When Mary learned she was going to give birth to the Messiah, she broke into song. The church has named her song the *Magnificat*. E. Stanley Jones, a Methodist theologian and missionary, once said that the *Magnificat* is the most revolutionary document in the world. Why would he say such a thing? When we first read it, it sounds like a young woman singing a simple song of praise to God. What's so revolutionary about that?

When we really pay attention to the words of Mary's song, though, we understand why Jones called it revolutionary. The *Magnificat* celebrates the fact that God chooses and uses people like Mary:

> With all my heart I glorify the Lord! In the depths of who I am I rejoice in God my savior. He has looked with favor on the low status of his servant. Look! From now on, everyone will consider me highly favored because the mighty one has done great things for me. Holy is his name. (Luke 1:46-49)

Mary sings her song of praise because she is in awe that God would use someone as ordinary as her. She is amazed that God has turned everything upside down. The rest of her song celebrates the strange way God has worked in the world. God "has pulled the powerful down from their thrones and lifted up the lowly" (v. 52). God "has filled the hungry with good things and sent the rich away empty-handed" (v. 53). The song is revolutionary because it reminds us of the unexpected ways God works and the unexpected people God uses—lowly, hungry, ordinary people such as Mary.

A Trail of Ordinary Women

You might remember that Matthew delivers the same truth in a subtle way at the beginning of his Gospel. Matthew begins with a genealogy: all of those "begats" that we typically skip over in the Bible. "So and so begat so and so, who begat so and so" is not exactly spellbinding reading! Former President Dwight Eisenhower said that everyone in his family was required to read the Bible through from time to time but that they were given permission to skip the genealogies.

Tucked away in Matthew's genealogy are five women—and women were almost never included in genealogies in the male-dominated first-century world. Matthew, though, inserted five women in Jesus' family tree, which is very surprising. Even more surprising are the five women he chose to include. He lists Tamar, who became pregnant by her father-in-law in Genesis 38. He mentions Rahab, a known harlot. He lists Ruth, a non-Jew from Moab. He includes Bathsheba, best remembered for her affair with King David. And he mentions Mary, a young peasant girl.

You would think if Matthew were going to insert women into Jesus' family tree that he would pick women of nobility, virtue, and great achievement. But Tamar, Rahab, Ruth, Bathsheba, and Mary? Those women are not exactly the kind of ancestors one would brag about. Their inclusion is quite a shock—and quite revolutionary itself. Matthew's genealogy reminds us of the same truth as Mary's song: God uses all kinds of people to accomplish the divine will. From these five ordinary, even sinful, women came Jesus, the promised Messiah.

The God of Abraham, Isaac, and Jacob

Matthew's genealogy subtly reveals the truth that Mary's song celebrates, but so does a common description of God the biblical writers use. They sometimes describe God as "the God of Abraham, Isaac, and Jacob." When the biblical writers use that phrase, they are reminding their readers that the God they are talking about is the same God who was revealed to these revered patriarchs.

When Peter, for example, tells a crowd in Acts 3 that "the God of Abraham, Isaac, and Jacob—the God of our ancestors—has glorified his servant Jesus" (v. 13), he is telling them that this is not a new God involved in the cross and resurrection but the same God who had already worked in their Jewish forefathers.

This phrase primarily has *historical* implications but, in light of Mary's song, we see that it also has *theological* implications. Abraham, Isaac, and Jacob were three very different men. Though they represent three generations of the same family, they had little in common. God was the God of each of them, though, and that is where this phrase intersects with the theme of Mary's song.

Abraham was a *superstar*. When the writer of the book of Hebrews mentions the heroes and heroines of faith in Hebrews 11, Abraham receives more notice than anyone else. In the eyes of the writer of Hebrews, Abraham was definitely one of the superstars of faith. Call it what you will—faith, obedience, commitment, or motivation—some people have it in spades. When that quality is hitched to opportunity, a superstar is born. These unusual people step out of the shadows to demand our attention and show us what real faith looks like. Since Abraham belongs at the top of the list as one of the superstars of faith, it is no surprise at all that God is "the God of Abraham."

Isaac, however, is another story. If Abraham could be called a superstar, Isaac could be dubbed a *nobody*. We actually know little about Isaac. He is remembered best as Abraham's son and Jacob's father. Beyond that, we don't know much. We do know that Abraham was willing to sacrifice him on the altar when he was a boy. We do know that his son, Jacob, hoodwinked him when he was an old man giving out the family blessing. That's about all we know about Isaac. He's a rather obscure figure in the Bible.

But here's the good news for any of us who fear we might never be numbered among the heroes and heroines of faith: God is the God of Isaac, too. God doesn't embrace just the superstar Abrahams of the world. The nobody Isaacs of the world are embraced, too.

The big surprise, though, is that God is "the God of Jacob." To put it bluntly, Jacob was a *scoundrel*. He cheated his brother Esau on two occasions, tricked Isaac into giving him the family blessing, and became a wealthy man by double-crossing his father-in-law, Laban. It seems that every time we meet Jacob in the book of Genesis, he's trying to con someone.

But one day Jacob had an experience that changed his life. He wrestled with a mysterious angel of God and had his name changed in the tussle. He became "Israel," gave up his conniving ways, and became a new man. That God would even pursue a scoundrel such as Jacob and want to bless him is a shocking idea.

That's the storyline of the Bible, though. God uses all kinds of people—the superstar Abrahams, the nobody Isaacs, and the scoundrel Jacobs. Whosoever will may come. The only prerequisite is the willingness to be used.

The Invitation to Dance

There is a song in *The Baptist Hymnal* (1975) called "Here Is My Life." It was written by Ed Seabough, and the words go like this:

Lord, you placed me in this world
Of time and space and missiles hurled,
With eyes I've seen the ghetto gloom;
With ears I've heard the sonic boom,
And man cry out for breathing room.

I cannot wait! I cannot wait!
Here is my life, I want to live it,
Here is my life, I want to give it
Serving my fellow man,
Doing the will of God;
Here is my life, Here is my life, Here is my life.

That's what Mary, for all of her ordinariness, was willing to say. Evidently, that's all God needs to hear. It's as if God invited her onto the dance floor and waited to see what she would say and do. Just because God offers an invitation doesn't mean a person will automatically say "yes." But Mary did, and the rest is history. When Mary received the divine invitation to dance, she said, "Here is my life."

If you think about it, it's surprising that Mary would even be able to sing her song of praise and celebrate God's goodness. This was, at best, an awkward and embarrassing situation for her. She didn't have a sonogram to verify anything. She didn't even have a husband to legitimize her pregnancy. All she had was a promise and this amazing notion that the God of the universe wanted to use her. But that was enough for her. Once she received the invitation, she headed for the dance floor, singing as she went.

Singing with Mary

Mary brings to mind all the other troubled, ordinary people God chooses and uses in the biblical story. It's an unlikely assortment of renegades and ragamuffins—not the kind of virtuous folks you would expect God to invite to the dance. In fact, as we read the biblical story we realize that often God called people not *because of* but *in spite of* who they are.

God chose Moses in spite of the fact that he had killed a man. God chose Rahab in spite of her work as a prostitute. God chose Ruth in spite of the fact that she wasn't even an Israelite. God chose David in spite of the fact that he was a simple shepherd boy. God chose Saul of Tarsus in spite of his persecution of Christians. God chose Simon Peter in spite of his volatile temperament. The list goes on and on.

The hope in that is obvious for all of us who feel like renegades and ragamuffins. If God used people like this in the past, perhaps God can use someone like us today. If, as Mary celebrates in her song, God has an affinity for people in spite of their shortcomings, perhaps God has a place for us in spite of our shortcomings, too. Even though we have two left feet, maybe God is inviting us onto the dance floor.

I love Mary's song because we all find ourselves in situations that are awkward, embarrassing, and uncertain. And we all feel, most of the time, unqualified for kingdom work. But if there are some changes going on in us, or around us, right now, Mary is a good role model. If our stomach is churning because of some big decision we're considering, we might want to follow Mary's lead. Who knows? Maybe the Holy Spirit has come upon us. Maybe that shadow hanging over us is the power of the Most High.

Sure, we would like all of the details—and a diagram showing how it will all work out. But since details and diagrams are usually in short supply, the operative questions are: Will we accept God's invitation to dance? Will we say, "Here is my life"? Will we go ahead and sing with Mary even though we don't know the end of the story?

As we face whatever we have to face this week, here's the blessing of the *Magnificat* for each of us: May our hearts glorify the Lord and our spirits rejoice in God our Savior. May we be assured that God has looked on us with great favor, even though we feel unqualified and of low status. From now on, others will know that we are the beloved of God because God has done great things for us. Holy is his name.

Shall we claim that—and sing that—with Mary?

God, sometimes we sense that you are calling us to take some risks, make some changes, and step up to some challenges. But too often we shy away, convinced that we're not up to the task. Give us, we pray, Mary's spirit. Use her song to renew and encourage us so that we will join you on the dance floor. Thank you for using ordinary people such as Mary—and us— to do your work in the world. We pray this in the name of Immanuel, Jesus our Lord. Amen.

Notes

Notes

3

ZECHARIAH'S SONG

Luke 1:57-58, 67-79

Central Question

How has God shone light in my darkness?

Scripture

Luke 1:57-58, 67-79 When the time came for Elizabeth to have her child, she gave birth to a boy. 58 Her neighbors and relatives celebrated with her because they had heard that the Lord had shown her great mercy.... 67 John's father Zechariah was filled with the Holy Spirit and prophesied, 68 "Bless the Lord God of Israel because he has come to help and has delivered his people. 69 He has raised up a mighty savior for us in his servant David's house, 70 just as he said through the mouths of his holy prophets long ago. 71 He has brought salvation from our enemies and from the power of all those who hate us. 72 He has shown the mercy promised to our ancestors, and remembered his holy covenant, 73 the solemn pledge he made to our ancestor Abraham. He has granted 74 that we would be rescued from the power of our enemies so that we could serve him without fear, 75 in holiness and righteousness in God's eyes, for as long as we live. 76 You, child, will be called a prophet of the Most High, for you will go before the Lord to prepare his way. 77 You will tell his people how to be saved through the forgiveness of their sins. 78 Because of our God's deep compassion, the dawn from heaven will break upon us, 79 to give light to those who are sitting in darkness and in the shadow of death, to guide us on the path of peace."

Reflecting

"I don't necessarily want to be famous when I grow up, but I would like to maybe work right below someone who is famous, or maybe several people who are famous." That was the career aspiration voiced to me by a student heading off to college. He was uncertain of his exact aspirations, but he didn't think he wanted the full brunt of celebrity, just a close taste of it. He thought he'd be fine as a No. 2 somewhere, but he really wanted to attach himself to a good No. 1.

That's what is developing for John the Baptist, even from his birth. This mission is clearly stated in the Gospel written by another John. When speaking of John the Baptist, John the apostle says, "He came as a witness to testify concerning the light, so that through him everyone would believe in the light. He himself wasn't the light, but his mission was to testify concerning the light" (John 1:7-8).

As someone who serves in a No. 2 role, I understand the unique challenges of being responsible but not entirely in charge. This is the fine line anyone has to walk as a vice president, second-in-command, or lieutenant. The first thing you have to know in such a role is that it's not about you. If you can handle that, there's a lot of opportunity for influence and leadership. And thus it was foretold of John the Baptist by the angel who spoke to his father: "He will bring many Israelites back to the Lord their God. He will go forth before the Lord, equipped with the spirit and power of Elijah.... He will make ready a people prepared for the Lord" (Luke 1:16-17).

From conception, John is portrayed as someone destined to point the way toward the light. That is no small task, because the people he will help are walking in darkness.

Studying

The words of Isaiah 9:2 echo throughout the Advent season, especially in Luke's narratives about the birth of Christ: "The people walking in darkness have seen a great light. On those living in a pitch-dark land, light has dawned." Much of Old Testament prophecy has to do with darkness being replaced by light, the empty being filled, the oppressed being set free. And so it should be no surprise that Luke's foreshadowing of the ministry of Jesus picks up this thread.

The hymn of praise in Luke 1:68-79 takes its most common title, *Benedictus* (or "blessed"), comes from the first word of its Latin translation. This is a customary word with which to begin a Jewish prayer: "Blessed be the Lord God of Israel" (see Ps 41:3; 72:18-19; 1 Chron 16:36; 2 Chron 2:12, etc.). Zechariah is a happy, doting father, but his attention initially focuses not on his child but on the Creator of all, the God of Israel.

What we see in this lesson's text, like last lesson's Song of Mary, is an example of ancient poetry, called a song for literary purposes. It is easy to see how Luke 1:67-79 forms a distinct unit that likely was dropped into Luke's Gospel narrative. As with the Song of Mary, it seems likely that, while Zechariah might have said something similar to this upon John's birth, the succinctly written poetry was honed and written down later. Of course, that doesn't make its witness any less true. In fact, we see in this passage an important bridge between Old Testament prophecies and the Gospel accounts of Jesus. The song shapes up as truthful when connected either backward or forward.

Zechariah had been struck speechless for nine months when he doubted the news of the angel who announced that his wife, Elizabeth, though barren for many years, would conceive and bear a son (1:20). His speech was restored only when John was born and Zechariah declared the name given by the angel. From this silence, Scripture says that Zechariah emerges "filled with the Holy Spirit" (1:67).

Luke may have intended Zechariah's period of silence to be representative of the silence that had fallen over Israel up to this time. Centuries had passed since the last recorded prophecy in the Old Testament, and expectations were high that surely God would redeem his people, Israel, from Roman oppression. At the time of John's birth, the Jews and their land were in disarray and uncertainty loomed. The darkness of which Isaiah spoke many years before became an apt metaphor once again.

According to a Jewish tradition, prophecy ceased with Malachi (c. 450 BC), not to be renewed until the messianic age. Others say prophecy first began to wane with Jeremiah (c. 600 BC)—although there were a few prophets who ministered after him. Another source states that prophecy ceased in the time of Alexander the Great (c. 330 BC). Various reasons for the cessation of prophecy are proposed: the people's sin, the destruction of the temple, or simply that the message of the prophets had been completed.

Zechariah had a long time to think about what he would say when his long-awaited son burst onto the scene. Don't you imagine he had rehearsed the words over and over in his mind, reflecting on what the angel had told him and what a miracle God had given him and Elizabeth? Note that even before Luke records this hymn of praise, he tells that, upon regaining his voice, Zechariah "began praising God" (v. 64).

Within the hymn, we hear Zechariah proclaim these things:

God is delivering the people from bondage (v. 68). This is a recurring theme of the Bible, and Zechariah jumps in that stream of prophets.

God has raised up a savior from the line of David (v. 69). This is also a connection to earlier prophecies. It is helpful for us to remember that we twenty-first-century Christians weren't the first to claim Jesus as the fulfillment of Old Testament prophecies. The Gospel writers and the Apostle Paul, in particular, lay this out from the beginning.

God has rescued Israel from the power of their enemies for a purpose: "so that we could serve him without fear" (v. 74). When salvation comes, it comes with a purpose, a mission, according to God's work in the world.

John will be called a prophet (v. 76), which quickly proves to be true. Furthermore, his role will be to "prepare [the] way" for

the Messiah. Even this work as Jesus' advance man produces the result of telling people how to be saved.

The light of heaven will dawn not because of what John is doing, and not because of what any human has done, but "because of our God's deep compassion" (v. 78).

The light that is coming will "guide us on the path of peace" (v. 79). This language is one of fourteen uses of the word "peace" in Luke's Gospel. Peace is a notable theme of Luke's writing and would have been seen as a valuable commodity among a continually occupied and oppressed people.

> Owing to this canticle's imagery of light and dawn, it is traditionally sung at morning prayer.

Zechariah's prophesy speaks in two directions: first in praise of God, then in description of who John will be and what he will do. John was going to be like a farmer preparing the land so that the soil would be ready to receive what was coming. Tilling land requires turning over the soil and breaking up the clods so the ground is soft enough for seeds to be planted there. By exposing Israel's sins and showing them the way of repentance, John would prepare them, softening the ground so they would be ready to receive the Messiah, who, in turn, would teach them about the importance of sowing seed on good soil.

Understanding

Life happens, and sometimes it doesn't happen the way we plan for it to or hope that it might. The story of Elizabeth and Zechariah illustrates the pain of a couple facing infertility, which in ancient times was considered to be the sign of a divine disapproval. Throughout the ages, humans have faced disappointment and anxiety mixed with hope and anticipation.

One such person was the poet Henry Wadsworth Longfellow. In 1863, during the height of the American Civil War, his oldest son, Charles, joined the Union army without his father's blessing. He was nineteen.

This was the year of the Battle of Gettysburg, where 40,000 men were killed, wounded, or went missing. Charles was severely wounded in November 1863 in the Battle of New Hope Church. Longfellow's wife had died two years earlier in a fire inside their home, and he was despondent over his family's woes. On Christmas Day 1863, Longfellow wrote the lyrics to "I Heard the Bells on Christmas Day," now a beloved Christmas carol.

An often-omitted fifth verse says, "It was as if an earthquake rent the hearth-stones of a continent, and made forlorn, the households born of peace on earth, good will to men." But the poem continues, just as we know it today: "Then pealed the bells more loud and deep, 'God is not dead, nor doth he sleep; the wrong shall fail, the right prevail, with peace on earth, good will to men.'"

Longfellow seemingly echoed the words of Zechariah: "Because of our God's deep compassion, the dawn from heaven will break upon us" (v. 78).

> When have you discovered light in the midst of your darkness?

What About Me?

• *Life is hard.* In his widely read book *The Road Less Traveled*, M. Scott Peck begins with the simple but profound statement that "life is difficult." And then he adds, "Once we truly know that life is difficult—once we truly understand and accept it—then life is no longer difficult" (15). Throughout the Bible, we see people of faith living in difficulty, facing huge challenges, and pleading with God to have mercy. Before we can truly appreciate the light that God can shine into our lives, we must come to grips with the darkness.

• *There are reasons for hope.* Christmas is a time of celebration and expectation, but not everyone gets what they want wrapped in a bright box with a bow. The carol "O Little Town of Bethlehem" had it right when speaking of the baby Jesus: "The hopes and fears of all the years are met in thee tonight." The Advent story is one of hope in the midst of pain, longsuffering, and waiting. Despite the darkness and difficulties of life, the light shines in the darkness.

• *God has helped us before.* This is a good reason to find reasons for hope. If God has seen us through dark times in the past, we can be more confident that God will see us through our current difficulties. When or where has God's light shined on your darkness before? Have you ever shared that story with anyone else? Doing so could be a gift in itself.

• *The light of God is worth celebrating.* Like Zechariah, we can praise God and help others to know how great God is. As in the *Benedictus*, this involves both an appreciation for how God has been at work globally ("He has come to help and has delivered his people," v. 68) and how God is working through individuals ("You, child, will be called a prophet of the Most High," v. 76).

• *The light of God's peace continues to shine.* The *Benedictus* calls us to walk in the path of peace brought about by Jesus and foreshadowed in the stories of Zechariah, Elizabeth, and John the Baptist. Consider these questions as Christmas approaches: What might you do to give a gift of peace this season? In what areas do you need to find peace, and what is one step you could take toward that result?

Resources

M. Scott Peck, *The Road Less Traveled*, 25th anniversary ed. (New York: Simon & Schuster, 2002).

Richard B. Vinson, *Luke*, Smyth & Helwys Bible Commentary (Macon GA: Smyth & Helwys, 2008).

ZECHARIAH'S SONG

Luke 1:57-58, 67-79

Introduction

When Jesus enters a life, there is reason to sing. At least, that's what Luke believed. He has everyone singing at the birth of Jesus. Mary has a song, Zechariah has a song, the angels have a song, and Simeon, the old priest in the temple, has a song.

This lesson, we listen to Zechariah's song. Zechariah, the father of John the Baptist, has an intriguing song to sing. But there is also an intriguing story behind his song. Before he gives us Zechariah's song, Luke tells us quite a bit about Zechariah's story.

Zechariah's Story

In Luke 1:5-25, Zechariah is introduced as a priest, a devout man who observed the Lord's commandments. He and his wife, Elizabeth, were getting on in years, and they had never been able to have a child. Then, like Mary, Zechariah received a visit from the angel Gabriel.

The angel told him that he and Elizabeth would have a son and that their son would be a special child. He would be a joy and a delight to them. He would be great in the Lord's eyes. He would bring many Israelites back to the Lord their God. And he would go before the Messiah and prepare the way for him.

Since both Zechariah and Elizabeth were quite old, this news came as a shock. It was so shocking, in fact, that Zechariah was dumbfounded. Literally, he couldn't speak. Luke writes, "Meanwhile, the people were waiting for Zechariah, and they wondered why he was in the sanctuary for such a long time. When he came out, he was unable to speak to them. They realized he had seen a vision in the temple, for he gestured to them and couldn't speak" (vv. 21-22).

Zechariah remained dumbfounded for nine months, Elizabeth's entire pregnancy. I wonder what it would be like to be silent for nine months. Certainly, an extended time of silence would probably be healing for all of us. We could all use some silence to escape the flood of words cascading around us every day. Proverbs 10:19 declares a truth we can all affirm: "With lots of words comes wrongdoing, but the wise restrain their lips." Restraining our lips sounds like a good idea in our wordy culture of noise and hype.

But nine months without uttering a word? That might be a little much. I once went to Laity Lodge in central Texas and learned about the Quiet House there. The Quiet House is a secluded cabin on the top of a hill that a person can reserve and use to escape the rat race. A person can become a modern-day Zechariah in the Quiet House and not say a word for a long time. I felt I needed a little "alone time" and considered reserving a spot for myself.

I wondered, though, even as I was getting the material from the folks at Laity Lodge, how long I would be able to remain quiet at the Quiet House. Just how long could I restrain my lips anyway? Nine months? Nine days? Nine hours? Probably more like nine minutes! Then the sound of all of that silence would make me start babbling to the rocks and trees. But Zechariah, Luke tells us, was silent for nine months: a silence he did not choose but had to endure.

There came the day, though, when Elizabeth gave birth to the baby boy they were expecting. She and Zechariah took him to be circumcised and to give him a name. Someone suggested they name the boy after his father. Zechariah Junior had a nice ring to it. Had that happened, we would be preaching and teaching about "Zechariah the Baptist" today. But Elizabeth didn't like that name at all. She said, "No, his name will be John" (v. 60).

Some insisted, though, and reminded her that no one in her family had that name. They turned to Zechariah and asked him what name he preferred. He asked for a writing tablet and wrote, "His name is John" (v. 63). He was as firm and straightforward as his wife. Immediately Zechariah was able to speak again and began praising God. His tongue was loosed, and out came the song we are listening to today.

That is Zechariah's story as Luke tells it in his Gospel. This story provides the necessary background for us to hear his song.

Two Stanzas

Zechariah's song has two stanzas. The first stanza is in verses 67-75. It praises God for finally sending the long-awaited Messiah. The second stanza (vv. 76-79) is addressed to John, the newborn baby who will be the forerunner of this Messiah.

Stanza One (1:67-75). Zechariah thanks God for coming to help his people, Israel. God is finally raising up a mighty savior from the house of David, just as had been prophesied long ago.

As Jews were prone to do in this era, Zechariah saw this Messiah as a political leader who would deliver Israel from its enemies and enable Israel to be free. But this freedom would enable Israel to serve God with a renewed passion, in holiness and righteousness. This first stanza of Zechariah's song is a grand celebration of God and God's willingness to send the long-promised Messiah to Israel.

Stanza Two (1:76-79). In the second stanza of his song, Zechariah tiptoes to the crib where his newborn son, John, lies and starts to sing to him. He tells John that he will be called a prophet of the Most High and that he will go before the Messiah to prepare the way. He tells his son that he will one day tell people how to be saved through the forgiveness of their sins. He celebrates the fact that this forgiveness will be possible because of the Light that is getting ready to come into the world. This Messiah will guide people into the path of peace, and Zechariah's boy, John, will be the one to introduce him to the world. The second stanza of Zechariah's song is a father's expression of hope and gratitude for the life of his newborn son.

In his commentary on Luke (Philadelphia: Westminster, 1953), William Barclay points out how much truth Zechariah packs into this second stanza of his song. Barclay says Zechariah perfectly captures the four steps along the Christian path:

• *Preparation.* Whether it is growing up in a Christian home, experiencing a personal tragedy, reading a random book on an airplane, or developing a relationship with a coworker, something or someone prepares us to meet and experience Jesus Christ. The seeds of a new life in Christ are planted at some point before we make the commitment to follow him.

• *Knowledge.* People simply didn't know what God was like until Jesus came. Jesus was the image of the invisible God, and knowledge of him and his way would lead people to God in John's day and in ours.

• *Forgiveness.* At the heart of both Zechariah's song and the Christian way is forgiveness. People sitting in the darkness of sin and guilt will see the light of forgiveness and freedom, and it's all possible because of the baby to be born in Bethlehem.

• *Peace.* A person who has taken those first three steps, who (1) is prepared to receive the good news of Christ, (2) has knowledge of his life, death, and resurrection, and (3) has experienced his freedom and forgiveness, will be led down the path of peace. The final step on the Christian way is what Jesus called "the abundant life."

Luke ends chapter 1 with a brief description of John's early life: "The child grew up, becoming strong in character. He was in the wilderness until he began his public ministry to Israel" (v. 80). John would become exactly what his father predicted: the forerunner of the Messiah, the one destined to prepare the way for his coming.

Go Ahead and Sing

What do you do when you've been unable to speak for nine months and suddenly can speak again? And what do you do when your wife gives birth to a baby boy when you were resigned to the fact that you would never have any children? Probably you do exactly what Zechariah did: you sing for joy. You forget your respectable reputation and carefully crafted image and start singing like a fool.

In his book *God Came Near* (Nashville TN: Thomas Nelson, 2004), Max Lucado tells the story of Bob Edens, who was blind for fifty-one years until a surgeon performed surgery on his eyes. Then, amazingly, he could see. This is what he said:

> I never would have dreamed that yellow is so...yellow. I don't have words. I am amazed by yellow. But red is my favorite color. I just can't believe red. I can see the shape of the moon, and I like nothing better than seeing a jet plane flying across the sky leaving a vapor trail. And, of course, sunrises and sunsets. And at night you look at the stars in the sky and the flashing light. You could never know how wonderful everything is. (Preface, xiii)

I don't know much about Bob Edens, but my guess is he sings a lot. When you've been in the darkness a long time, and suddenly there is light, you have to sing. And when you have been in silence a long time, like Zechariah, and suddenly you can speak, you have to sing.

It is possible, even probable, that some of us are sitting in some kind of darkness today, enveloped in some kind of personal silence. Perhaps it's a quiet grief that we can't articulate to anyone. Perhaps it's a nagging worry, or a constant confusion, or even a keen awareness of the absence of God. For whatever reason, we find ourselves sitting in some kind of personal darkness, unable to speak.

The promise of God to everyone with even a mustard-seed-sized faith is this: beyond every death there is a resurrection. Things within us and around us will inevitably die. Relationships will die, concepts of God will die, and hopes and dreams will die, too. But on the other side of all of these deaths, there is something new, something better. If the resurrection of Jesus means anything at all to our everyday lives, it is exactly at this point.

Beyond every death there is a resurrection.

Beyond every darkness there is a light.

And beyond every silence there is a song.

Conclusion

Next lesson, we will hear the most famous of Luke's Christmas songs: the song of the angels announcing Jesus' birth. It is an upbeat chorus of praise, filled with good news. The angels' song will give us the opportunity to remember how good our good news really is.

But this lesson, let's not overlook the good news in Zechariah's song. It, too, can fill us with hope and shed some light into any dark situation we might be experiencing. If you happen to be sitting in darkness, unable to articulate your feelings, Zechariah's song promises that there is coming a day when light will shine again. There is coming a day when your mouth will be opened and your tongue will be loosed. When that happens, remember old, mute Zechariah, forget your staid respectability, and go ahead and sing.

Sometimes, God, we feel just like Zechariah: overwhelmed by what has happened to us and unable to express exactly how we feel. Give us the faith to sit in the darkness until light comes. And give us the courage to bear the silence until we can speak again. Make us sensitive, too, to the people around us who are sitting in some kind of dark silence. This we pray in the name of the one about whom Zechariah sang, Jesus the Messiah and our Lord. Amen.

Notes

Notes

4

THE ANGELS' SONG

Luke 2:8-14

Central Question

How can I experience God's peace this Christmas?

Scripture

Luke 2:8-14 Nearby shepherds were living in the fields, guarding their sheep at night. 9 The Lord's angel stood before them, the Lord's glory shone around them, and they were terrified. 10 The angel said, "Don't be afraid! Look! I bring good news to you—wonderful, joyous news for all people. 11 Your savior is born today in David's city. He is Christ the Lord. 12 This is a sign for you: you will find a newborn baby wrapped snugly and lying in a manger." 13 Suddenly a great assembly of the heavenly forces was with the angel praising God. They said, 14 "Glory to God in heaven, and on earth peace among those whom he favors."

Reflecting

As a young teenager, I read a book about angels written by Billy Graham. Years later, I still recall vividly how scary parts of that book seemed to me.

The evangelist's description of some possible angelic visitations—including a little girl in a raincoat appearing mysteriously on a roadway, or something like that—scared me as much as a horror movie. Years later, an adult friend recounted to me an experience she had as a child when she believes an angel nudged her in the night, prompting her to go see her mother on the night her mother died. I slept lightly for weeks, fearful of an angelic nudge in the night.

When Luke 2:9 says the shepherds were terrified by the glory of the Lord, we may easily understand why. Visitations by angels count as supernatural events. Even if we perceive that angels are the "good guys," most of us at some level are frightened by the supernatural; it doesn't matter if it comes from a good or evil source.

A sudden surprise doesn't even have to be supernatural. I've been known to jump and shriek when a friend surprises me from behind or around a corner.

Think of the angelic visitations in the Gospel birth narratives in terms of a close encounter with forces beyond human understanding. In each case, the angels' message includes a command, "Don't be afraid" (Matt 1:20; Luke 1:13, 30; 2:10). While the thrust of the Song of the Angels in this lesson's text is wholly positive and celebratory, it nevertheless begins with a jolt. Shepherds were doing what shepherds do, minding their own business, probably trying to keep warm, and then—bam!— out of nowhere angels appear. We can imagine hearts racing, adrenaline rushing, and eyes widening in disbelief. The Greek phrase in verse 9 translated "they were terrified" would be more literally rendered "they feared a great fear."

> Angels are often depicted in Scripture as supernatural warriors. That is the meaning behind the divine title "Lord of Hosts," namely, God as the commander of an angelic "host" or army. The archangel Michael, in particular, is commonly depicted in later Christian tradition as a powerful, warlike protector (see Dan 10:13; Jude 9; Rev 12:7-9).

Before we rush to the celebration of the baby Jesus, let us stop and identify with the frightened shepherds. The Bible's first announcement of this news of peace began anything but peacefully.

Studying

Charles Jennens constructed the libretto for Handel's *Messiah*, an oratorio that tells the overarching story of God's redemptive plan through Jesus Christ. Jennens masterfully wove together dozens of Old and New Testament passages to create the libretto, which he in turn handed off to Handel to set to music.

Curiously, in Jennens's form, he skips directly from the prophecy of Isaiah 9 to the story of the shepherds in Luke 2. He doesn't specifically tell about the birth of the Messiah in a work that is named *Messiah*. He omits the first seven verses of Luke 2 and jumps directly to our text for this lesson. If you're purporting to tell the story of the Messiah, why might you skip the details of the birth of the Messiah and go straight to the announcement of his birth? Perhaps the answer is because the declaration of what has happened is so much more powerfully told by the angels.

Handel portrays the story well at this point. He begins with a rather peaceful musical treatment of the line, "There were shepherds abiding in the field, keeping watch over their flock by night." Then he immediately plunges the soprano soloist into a fast-paced recitative with the news of the angels: "And lo! The angel of the Lord came upon them" (v. 9). The music startles.

The angels' song is traditionally known as *Gloria in excelsis*, Latin for "Glory in the highest [i.e., to God]."

The shepherds clearly were startled by the appearance of the angels. I suspect we would have been, too. The curious thing is that they didn't have any reason we know of to be expecting news from God. Often, even when we are praying urgently for divine direction, we seem not to be expecting news from God, either. How often do we really expect to hear from God—even when we pray? And how perceptive are we to hear God's voice amid the routines of life? Do we see the signs God puts in front of us even when we're not looking for signs?

Our tendency to be startled by God reminds me of a beautiful old hymn:

Sometimes a light surprises the Christian while he sings;
It is the Lord who rises with healing in his wings:
When comforts are declining, he grants the soul again
a season of clear shining, to cheer it after rain.

The "manger" of verse 12 is perhaps the most famous piece of furniture in the Bible. Modern understanding of exactly what kind of conditions Mary and Joseph landed in have changed a bit from what many of us were taught in Sunday school years ago. Stop for a moment and notice that the text does not mention any animals being present, yet we assume animals were present because the label given to the place where Jesus was born. Maybe animals were present, and maybe they weren't. The animals aren't the point of the story, and neither is the manger. The manger serves as an identifying mark for the shepherds as they follow the guidance of the angels.

Modern archaeology leads scholars to believe that this stable might have been an interior room of a house, perhaps a cave-like room situated underneath a family's humble living quarters. It would have been the kind of place that could have housed animals indoors when needed, or it could have been used for other purposes. If we were to cast this space in a modern-day adaptation of Luke's account, we would perhaps do well to set the action in the street-level garage of a split-level house.

The angels gave the shepherds directions by telling them what they would see when they arrived. The manger references of Luke 1 might echo the theme of Deuteronomy 8:3, where Moses said we can't live on bread alone. Those words, of course, were repeated by Jesus during his temptation in the wilderness (Luke 4:4). Later on, Jesus portrays himself as "the bread of life" (John 6:35). The manger, the feeding trough, where baby Jesus was laid, became a sign to the shepherds and foreshadowed the sign of Jesus' true mission as the bread of heaven.

Immediately after writing the paragraph above, I stopped for a few minutes to check on friends via Facebook. To my surprise, I saw there a post from my friend Samira Izadi Page, who operates a ministry to immigrant families in Dallas called Gateway of Grace. A former Muslim from Iran who became a Christian through our Baptist church and later was ordained as an Episcopal priest, Samira seeks to offer others the kind of

> Who except God can give you peace? Has the world ever been able to satisfy the heart?
> —Gerard Majella

hospitality she and her family knew upon arrival in the United States.

Here's what she had just posted:

> Had a few of Gateway of Grace friends over for lunch after they had gone to church with us. We took them to St. John's Episcopal Church. She told me that she had seen that church and those people in a dream a few years ago and in that dream the guys in red gave her bread and red water! As a Muslim woman, she would have had no way of knowing Communion Episcopal style.

The added irony here is that Samira, as a young girl living in Iran, saw a vision of Mary and did not know whom she was seeing. She described the woman in her vision to her Muslim mother, who understood that this was Mary, of the Christian Bible. But it was not until Samira arrived in Dallas years later that she understood the meaning of her own vision when she learned about the mother of our Lord.

Likewise, the shepherds couldn't have known the symbolism of what they saw that night or the meaning of the directions given by the angels. And yet both the sight and the symbol were pregnant with meaning.

Understanding

Sometimes a light surprises. None of us can fully anticipate what God has in store for us and those close to us. Nor can we manipulate God to produce the outcomes we would like to see. And yet we find over time that God is full of surprises. This theme is played out time and again in the Bible, and many believers through the ages bear testimony to it as well. Remember that "nothing is impossible for God" (Luke 1:37).

Compared to how humans normally look at things, God's view of the world is upside down. The "good news to the poor" (Luke 4:18) that Jesus

As heavenly angels offer praise to God, they also announced peace for humans, whom God blesses; this includes "all people" who accept this baby's birth as "wonderful, joyous news" (Luke 2:10). **110 NT**

proclaims is woven into the fabric of the Gospels, beginning with Jesus' birth. The shocking news of God's redemptive plan is that God's ways are not our ways, and our ways are not God's ways.

Linus was right. In the classic TV special *A Charlie Brown Christmas,* the humble and overlooked Linus steals the show when, amid everyone else's capitulation to commercialism, Charlie Brown shouts, "Isn't there anyone who knows what Christmas is all about?"

The spotlight falls on Linus, and he recites the very words of our Scripture passage this lesson from Luke 2.

Then he adds, "That's what Christmas is all about, Charlie Brown."

What About Me?

• *Have you ever met an angel?* Maybe not in the same way the shepherds did, but have you ever sensed the presence of divine power or comfort or peace in a time of great need? What people or events have been the bearers of a message from God to you?

• *How has the light of God surprised you?* Few can boast of angelic visitations. Whatever your experience of the supernatural, however, there likely are times when God's grace has come into your life in surprising ways. Remember that the shepherds weren't expecting to see an angelic choir or hear their proclamation of good news. So it often is with us: God shows up when we least expect it! Reflect on those experiences this week as you prepare for Christmas with gratitude.

• *What leads you to think you are unworthy to bear the message of hope in Christ?* What are the areas of brokenness or wounded self-esteem or lesser social status that you think make you inferior to others? Consider what God did through the shepherds, who were more lowly than anyone reading this lesson today, and allow God's Spirit to reveal your true worthiness.

• *What does peace have to do with Christmas?* The days leading up to Christmas can be the most hectic and frustrating time of the

year. How can we find peace in the midst of overbooked sched-
ules, travel, and the strain on our bank accounts from
gift-buying, entertaining, and other holiday activities? How can
we receive the angels' message of peace when Christmas has worn
us out?

• *What would an announcement of peace on earth mean for you today?*
And how might your peace be tied to the peace of others? Think
this week of those to whom you might offer the gift of peace, and
in return you might find peace yourself.

Resources

"Sometimes a Light Surprises," *The Cyber Hymnal* <http://cyberhymnal.org/htm/s/o/m/sometime.htm>.

Richard B. Vinson, *Luke*, Smyth & Helwys Bible Commentary (Macon GA: Smyth & Helwys, 2008)

THE ANGELS' SONG

Luke 2:8-14

Introduction

The overwhelming emotion in the angels' song is joy. This is a song of good news: "wonderful, joyous news for all people" (Luke 2:10). The melody to this song must have been bouncy and festive, the kind of tune that makes even reluctant feet start tapping. This melody lifted spirits and made people want to dance.

We Christians need to hear the angels' song occasionally just to remember that this message about Jesus really is wonderful, joyous news for all people. Sadly, it's always a temptation to forget that. Several years ago, I wrote a book titled *Making the Good News Good Again* (Macon GA: Smyth & Helwys, 2009) because I sensed a pressing need in my own life for that to happen. It is so easy to lose the good news in a pile of religious rules, church obligations, and boring doctrines.

Regrettably, for many people in our society, the word "church" conjures up negative images. Many people don't think of church as a place of joy and celebration where they can be healed, but rather they see it as a place of boredom and bickering where they will wither and die. When they think of the church, they think of bad news, not good news.

How we Christians need to hear the angels' song! How we need to recover "wonderful, joyous news for all people!" (v. 10). The reason the gospel is such good news is captured in this one phrase in the angels' song: "Your savior is born today in David's city. He is Christ the Lord" (v. 11). Of all of the needs we have in our lives, God thought we most needed a Savior. The arrival of that Savior is the reason we and the angels sing.

The Need for a Savior

When we think about the people we need in our lives to be happy and healthy, we can come up with quite a list. A psychiatrist is indispensable when we're struggling with an emotional issue. A doctor is crucial to our well-being when we're physically ill. A friend is a godsend when we're going through trouble. A pastor is invaluable when we have spiritual questions. A lawyer is essential if we have legal matters to address. We have all kinds of needs, and, fortunately, we have all kinds of people who can help us meet those needs. But God perceived that our biggest need of all was for a Savior.

Imagine that you are walking along, minding your own business, when you suddenly and unexpectedly fall into a pit of quicksand. Slowly you start to sink, and the harder you try to escape the clutches of that quicksand, the faster you sink. Frankly, it looks pretty bleak for you when, to your relief, you see a group of people running toward you, seemingly to give you help. Soon you are encircled by a posse of Good Samaritans, but you can scarcely believe what happens next.

One person in the group begins to criticize you for falling in the quicksand. "How could you have been so careless? Any normal person would have seen that pit and walked around it. What were you thinking? You deserve to be in the quicksand because you're just reaping what you have sown." You immediately decide to tune this "helper" out because, even though you know some of what he says is true, he's not doing anything at all to get you out of the quicksand.

The second person in the posse begins to explain to you the chemical composition of the sand you're stuck in. "It will be helpful," she says in her analytical voice, "if you understand your surroundings." But, even as she speaks, you know that she is not going to do anything to rescue you either. Understanding your surroundings is not going to help you escape your surroundings.

The next person steps forward and offers you a quick course on dealing with stress. He gives you four keys for handling stressful situations, exhorts you to breathe deeply, and invites you to meditate for a while. Then he tells you that, in the midst of any kind of anxiety, you need to develop some hobbies and other outside interests. You can only roll your eyes in disbelief as you sink a little deeper into the quicksand.

Another person steps forward to try to convince you that you are not really in quicksand at all. It looks like quicksand, feels like quicksand, and will soon taste like quicksand, but you need to think positive thoughts, and everything will be fine. You create your own reality by how you think, he says confidently. But you know, in your heart of hearts, that positive thinking is not going to get you out of the quicksand.

Frankly, by this time, things are looking hopeless. This posse of "helpers" has turned out to be a posse of charlatans. What they're peddling won't get you out of your predicament.

Then, to your great excitement, you look beyond this group of hucksters and see a lone runner coming toward you. He has a rope in his hand and determination on his face. He throws the rope to you and starts to lift you out of the quicksand. He doesn't say much. He just pulls and pulls until you are finally out of the quicksand and standing on firm ground. You stand there panting and exhausted, filled with gratitude for your savior. Finally, a true helper came to your rescue. Finally, someone did something that addressed your problem.

That's the Christian gospel in a nutshell. When we were helpless and hopeless, God came to our rescue. God gave us a Savior to lift us out of our sin. There is an old gospel hymn, "Love Lifted Me," that cuts to the heart of it:

I was sinking deep in sin, far from the peaceful shore,
Very deeply stained within, sinking to rise no more.
But the Master of the sea heard my despairing cry,
From the waters lifted me, now safe am I.

Love lifted me. Love lifted me.
When nothing else could help, love lifted me.

That's what we remember and celebrate when we hear the angels' song. Love showed up just when we needed it most. When nothing else could help, love lifted us. And it showed up in the most surprising way imaginable—as a baby wrapped in swaddling clothes and lying in a manger.

An Unlikely Rescuer

When we're down there in the pit looking for a rescuer, we assume that if one shows up he or she will be impressive and powerful. Our savior will be a military leader, a Navy SEAL, a police officer trained in rescue operations, or a bodybuilder capable of pulling heavy objects to safety. But incredibly, our Savior shows up as a baby in a bed of straw.

Some people just couldn't buy that idea in the first-century world. They saw it as heretical that anyone would think that the God of the universe would come into the world that way. And thirty years later, the cross of Christ became an even bigger scandal. When the early church started saying that God showed up as a baby in Bethlehem and died as a criminal outside of Jerusalem, it was a tough sell. Not many people in that day could grasp that kind of God.

When the Apostle Paul wrote to the Corinthians, he acknowledged that this kind of God was a scandal to the Jews and foolishness to the Gentiles (1 Cor 1:18-25). It seems to be that way even in our day. A God who shows up as a baby and dies as a criminal is not exactly the kind of God most modern people are looking for. This God is too vulnerable and powerless for modern tastes.

In *From Death to Birth* (Philadelphia: Fortress, 1973), Edmund Steimle writes:

> When God comes to us he does not overwhelm. He plays it cool. Low key. He always appears to be less than he really is, what someone called "the ironical man." Like a child born in a stable. Like a young man growing up in a family unrecognized for what he really is. Like a prisoner refusing to answer the false accusations of a judge. Like a man riding bareback on a donkey, his heels grabbing the belly of the animal to keep from falling off. God always seems to be less than he really is. (71)

That aspect of God's character is frustrating at times. We wish God would be more widescreen and Technicolor. We wish God wouldn't hide as a baby in a bed of straw or as a man dying on a cross between two thieves. But God always seems to be less than he really is, which means God will typically come to us in the context of our everyday lives and move in the quiet places of our heart. God will not force, push, shove, or shout. God will come to the door and knock—and wait for a response.

After we do respond, the challenge we all have is to keep hearing the angels' song. Our gospel is good news of great joy. We have to keep knowing that and trusting in that. More importantly, we need to keep declaring that in the way we live. By our words and actions, we say to those around us, "I bring good news to you—wonderful, joyous news for all people" (v. 10).

When Religion Gets Heavy

When we find ourselves unable to sing with the angels, it's time to realize something is wrong. When we feel burdened by our faith, start dreading church obligations, and sense we are just going through the motions with God, we should see a big red flag waving before our eyes. Our heaviness is trying to tell us something important. It's trying to tell us that religion has sapped us of our joy.

I've read Matthew 11:28 for years and have always found it to be a comforting verse: "Come to me, all you who are struggling hard and carrying heavy loads, and I will give you rest." I've typically interpreted Jesus' words in that verse as directed to people burdened by the pressures and worries of everyday life. I've interpreted them to say, "If you're worn out from too much stress, and burdened by the worries of your daily existence, come to me and find rest." And I still think that verse applies to people who are stressed out by life.

But lately I've started reading that verse with new eyes. I've started seeing it as directed to weary Christians who no longer find it possible to sing with the angels. I'm thinking that it is directed to tired preachers, burned-out deacons, weary Sunday school teachers, and angry fundamentalists. I hear Jesus saying to all of us, "Come to me and find another way. Quit struggling and straining. Quit trying so hard. Rest in my grace and forgiveness. Relax for a change and enjoy being held."

In other words, I've started seeing Matthew 11:28 as an invitation to weary Christians to quit feeling so responsible. I've started hearing that verse as Jesus' invitation to me, and people like me, to start singing the angels' song.

Conclusion

Eugene Peterson writes,

> The word Christian means different things to different people. To one person it means a stiff, upright, inflexible way of life, colorless and unbending.... But if we get our information from the biblical material, there is no doubt that the Christian life is a dancing, leaping, daring life. (*Traveling Light* [Downer's Grove IL: InterVarsity, 1982] 57)

If nothing else, hearing the angels' song ought to remind us of that truth. We have a gospel of incredibly good news, filled with joy for all people. Once that gospel soaks down into the depths of who we are, we can't help but live a dancing, leaping, daring life.

Thank you, God, for good news of great joy. Forgive us when we garble that message and fall into a religion that is burdensome and boring. Restore unto us the joy of our salvation so that we can sing with the angels. This we pray in the name and spirit of Christ, our Lord. Amen.

Notes

Notes

5

SIMEON'S SONG
Luke 2:25-35

Central Question

How are my deepest longings fulfilled in Jesus?

Scripture

Luke 2:25-35 A man named Simeon was in Jerusalem. He was righteous and devout. He eagerly anticipated the restoration of Israel, and the Holy Spirit rested on him. 26 The Holy Spirit revealed to him that he wouldn't die before he had seen the Lord's Christ. 27 Led by the Spirit, he went into the temple area. Meanwhile, Jesus' parents brought the child to the temple so that they could do what was customary under the Law. 28 Simeon took Jesus in his arms and praised God. He said, 29 "Now, master, let your servant go in peace according to your word, 30 because my eyes have seen your salvation. 31 You prepared this salvation in the presence of all peoples. 32 It's a light for revelation to the Gentiles and a glory for your people Israel." 33 His father and mother were amazed by what was said about him. 34 Simeon blessed them and said to Mary his mother, "This boy is assigned to be the cause of the falling and rising of many in Israel and to be a sign that generates opposition 35 so that the inner thoughts of many will be revealed. And a sword will pierce your innermost being too."

Reflecting

Children are the picture of anticipation at Christmas, aren't they? And then, as the saying goes, "Nothing's over like Christmas." Sometimes the hype doesn't match the results.

My wife and I have twin sons who now are young adults. It's interesting to remember our boys' younger days and see how they have miraculously matured and changed. I recently ran across a blog my wife, Alison, and I wrote when the boys were in fifth grade (which, unfortunately, is no longer available online). Alison wrote:

> **?** Do you experience an emotional let-down after Christmas? Why do you think that is?

> Some of my friends have complained that they don't know what to get their kids because their kids haven't given them many ideas about what they want for Christmas. That hasn't been a problem in our household. Garrett's list is so long I told him it ought to count for the next three Christmases and birthdays combined. And Luke's list isn't coming up short either. To make things worse, they keep discovering more things they want to add as they pore over each new catalog or newspaper ad. I told them enough is enough—they're not going to get everything on their lists as it is, so why add more to it?

In response, I added these words:

> Even though we have told the boys several major items on their lists are absolutely out of the question, that does not deter their ability to hope. Having only this year allowed Game Boys—and having regretted it on more than one occasion—I'm not keen to move on to the further distraction of GameCubes and XBoxes. So Luke and Garrett try to work every angle imaginable.
>
> "What if someone gave us an XBox?" one of them asks periodically. "Would you let us keep it?" Or "What if we won a GameCube?" the other chimes in. "We'd have to take it, wouldn't we?" The fact that neither of those things is going to happen bears no restraint on their anticipation that it could. Sometimes, we adults can learn from this boundless hope, especially when it's applied in the service of others.

We have a friend at church who has come to Texas from Burundi, fleeing political persecution. He left behind his wife and family to save his life, and now he's struggling to make ends meet in our economic downturn. This week, he started a new part-time job working nights at Target. We are all excited about his new opportunity, even though it's not as much income as he really needs. Nevertheless, Luke has prayed for our friend with great enthusiasm, remembering him every night for more than a week. He is asking God to help our friend become employee of the month at Target and get an immediate promotion. That is faith with anticipation. And a reminder that children sometimes know better than we that with God all things are indeed possible.

Studying

We see in the biblical character Simeon someone who truly understands anticipation. He was clinging on to life as an old man, waiting for the consolation of Israel. Somehow, some way, he had faith that endured into old age. That's a rare trait, because many of us tend to become more cynical as we age. The older we get, the harder it is to believe.

> The traditional name of this canticle is *Nunc dimittis*, from the first words of the Latin text.

By the way, new medical research shows a correlation between cynicism and dementia (Christensen). The more negative your attitude, the more likely you are to suffer from dementia. Simeon obviously was a positive person to be able to hope as diligently as he did for as long as he did.

What Simeon anticipated is described as "the restoration of Israel" (v. 25). On an immediate level, that likely meant he hoped that God would remove Israel's Roman occupiers. But this idea also connects to the hopes of Hebrew prophets for generations, most notably expressed in the words of Isaiah 40:1-2:

Comfort, comfort my people! says your God. Speak compassionately to Jerusalem, and proclaim to her that her compulsory service has ended, that her penalty has been paid, that she has received from the Lord's hand double for all her sins!

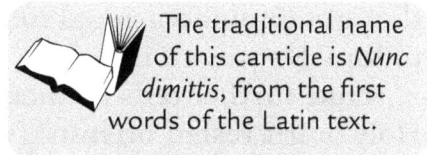

Throughout the ages, the Hebrew people had known slavery and occupation, had been chastised by the Lord for their sin, and sought restoration. This history plays out in the Bible on both corporate and individual levels. The psalms exemplify both.

The description of Simeon as "righteous and devout" (v. 25) tells us that he followed the Torah and did his best to lead a holy life. In modern Christian parlance, he would be someone who read his Bible daily, prayed, and went to church every time the doors were open. Faith was not an after-thought or an occasional interest to him. He was all in.

Luke further tells us that "the Holy Spirit rested on him" (v. 25). This is an interesting description that has fuller meaning when we consider that Luke wrote this account years after it happened,

> Simeon, like Zechariah and Elizabeth, was *righteous* (careful to obey the commandments) and *devout* (he led a God-focused life). *restoration*: echoes passages like Isaiah 40:1-2; 49:13; 51:3, which refer to God rescuing God's people from their exile in Babylon and restoring them to Judea. Simeon, like Zechariah, hopes God will drive the Romans out of Palestine (Luke 1:71, 74). *Holy Spirit rested on him*: He is a prophet, like Elizabeth (Luke 1:41), Zechariah (Luke 1:67), and Anna (Luke 2:36). **110 NT**

after the early church knew explicitly the power of the Holy Spirit from the day of Pentecost forward. For Luke to look backward and say the Holy Spirit "rested" on Simeon carries more profound meaning than if this description had been given before Pentecost. Luke knew the real power of the Holy Spirit as it guided the apostles and others in miraculous ways that Luke himself would record in the book of Acts.

We may think of Simeon as a warm and inspirational charac-ter, but closer examination might cause us to see him more as an eccentric, someone not likely to be invited to a dinner party. Simeon gives the impression of being part fortune-teller, part prophet, and part mystic. When people believe they have heard directly from God that they will not die until something in particular happens, most of us normal folks get suspicious. Is this guy nuts? Does he have mental problems? We assume that a spiritual experience that isn't normative for us can't be real. Such

an assumption cuts off the power of God to be more than we will let God be. There is danger in creating God in our own image.

Of all the beautiful words in this story, my favorite is verse 28: "Simeon took Jesus in his arms and praised God." If I were a visual artist, this is the scene I would paint. A modern Christian artist named Ron DiCianni has indeed painted this scene in watercolors, producing a stunning visual that tells a story. We see only the old man Simeon and the swaddled baby. Simeon has his head thrown back, eyes closed and mouth open in amazement, a tear falling from his eye.

The artist wrote about his inspiration:

In this painting I tried to let Simeon's face tell the story. Ecstasy. I have a feeling Simeon clutched that baby like no other. He knew that he held the "light" of the world, which I symbolized by the star emanating from the Baby. Intertwined through them both, I put a map of the world with its obvious symbolism that Christ came to impact the whole world, and not just the Jews, as most of the people would have concluded. Those lands, like North and South America, as well as others, were not even known to Simeon's world, but God knew all along that you and I would need a Savior. Simeon's tear was put in to reflect deep joy. But the more I contemplated it, the more I realized it could symbolize that Simeon also might have known that this Baby was born to be crucified. That was why he came. ("Simeon's Moment")

In this moment, Simeon declares what we might paraphrase in Texas like this: "I'm good now. I've seen all I need to see. I can die in peace." There is in Simeon's declaration both an affirmation and a letting go. God has done what God promised to do, and there is nothing more Simeon need do. This is a beautiful reminder of the all-sufficiency of God's provision, harkening back to Abraham and Isaac, when God provided the lamb for the sacrifice (Gen 22). The fulfillment of God's promise required no action on Simeon's part other than steadfast belief

Understanding

Christmas Day has passed. But it will come again, and we'll repeat all the singing and the storytelling, all the eating and the gathering. Why do we keep repeating this pattern year after year? For Christians who observe the Advent season, anticipation and expectation are mainstays. Every year, we choose to act like we don't know how the story is going to end, and yet we do. It's the same story. But by forcing ourselves to postpone the celebration, we remind ourselves of the importance of waiting. In this practice, we learn patience (not a virtue to some of us) and dependency.

From the perspective of opening presents, it's true that "nothing's over like Christmas." When the wrapping paper and bows are strewn all over the floor, all has been revealed and there is nothing left to wonder about. But is that all there is?

Our task today is not to set aside the wonder of Christmas just because a day on the calendar has passed. We must gather up the wrappings of Christmas—the stories, the songs, the spirit of giving, the wonder of receiving—and apply them in each of the days ahead, beginning with today.

Maybe you didn't get what you really wanted for Christmas this year. Or maybe you have so much that you didn't want anything at all. The message of Simeon is not simply, "There's always next year." Rather, the message may be, "There's all of this year." There's a full new year of living in anticipation of what God can and will do among us. There's a full new year of hoping for the kingdom of God to be made known on earth as it is in heaven.

What About Me?

• *In our materialistic world, not much attention is paid to deep longings.* All around us, attention is called to things that are merely surface deep. The canticles of Christmas in this study have called us to think beyond that shallowness. We have been challenged to expect great things from God and to attempt great things for God. We have been called to hear the songs of angels and to believe that with God, all things are possible.

• *What is the most audacious thing God could do before your eyes in your lifetime?* Seriously: what is the most outrageous thing you could begin to pray for that would demonstrate God's saving work in the world? What harm could there be in beginning to pray toward that end?

• *What will you carry forward from Christmas?* What have you gained that will last longer than the batteries in a child's new toy? What happens next? As you reflect on these five lessons and on your Christmas celebrations—the music you've heard, the sermons you've heard, the stories you've shared with family and friends— what is one thing you can cling to that will sustain you through the year ahead?

• *How many of the things you usually thank God for benefit only you?* What can you thank God for that expresses gratitude for more than merely your own interests? We learn from Simeon the joy of seeing God fulfill a dream that benefits all people. That's a reminder that should guide our prayer lives as well.

Resources

Jen Christensen, "Cynicism Linked to Greater Dementia Risk, Study Says," CNN.com, 29 May 2014 <http://www.cnn.com/2014/05/28/health/cynical-dementia/>.

"Simeon's Moment," ChristCenteredMall.com <http://www.christcenteredmall.com/stores/art/dicianni/simeons-moment.htm>

Richard B. Vinson, *Luke*, Smyth & Helwys Bible Commentary (Macon GA: Smyth & Helwys, 2008).

SIMEON'S SONG

Luke 2:25-35

Introduction

The happiest times in my life have been when I was waiting expectantly for something to happen. I'm thinking, for example, of the months leading up to the births of our children. Every doctor's appointment Sherry had was exciting. We talked about names, planned the nursery, went to birthing classes, and dreamed about how our child would look and act. Her pregnancies were exciting, happy times for us because they were filled with so much expectation.

I'm thinking, too, of the birth of books. How exciting the publishing process has always been for me. It is filled with a waiting that is both agonizing and exciting. During those pre-publication months, I'm living on tiptoe waiting for things to happen. I'm waiting for the contract to arrive, waiting for the proofs to be sent, waiting to see the cover design, and waiting for the actual publication of the book. The entire publishing process is fun because it is filled with expectation.

There was once a line in the "Peanuts" comic strip where Charlie Brown said, "Happiness is having three things to look forward to and nothing to dread." I think Charlie hit the nail squarely on the head, don't you?

We come this lesson to the Sunday after Christmas and the last of the four songs in the Gospel of Luke. It's Simeon's song, a song of hope. Simeon has been living on tiptoe, waiting for the arrival of the promised Messiah. When he goes to the temple one day and sees Mary and Joseph and their baby, he knows his dream has finally come true. He takes Jesus in his arms and starts to sing for joy because he can now depart this life in peace. He has seen the promised one. He knows that this baby will be a light of God's revelation to Jews and Gentiles alike.

Sometimes we say, "As long as there's life, there's hope," but we could just as easily say, "As long as there's hope, there's life." Old Simeon in the temple had a hope that kept him alive. The Living Bible says, "He was constantly expecting the messiah to come soon" (Luke 2:25). That expectation probably got him out of bed every morning. But that hope is not automatic. Hope is fragile, and it can even die.

When Hope Dies

Let me tell you about Mrs. Dollahon, who ran a grocery store in Andice, the little town in Texas where I was pastor during my seminary days. There were two general stores in Andice: Jacob's and Dollahon's. But, for all practical purposes, there was only one store in town. Everyone shopped at Jacob's, a true country store where you could buy everything from fresh sausage to overalls to nuts and bolts.

Dollahon's was run by Mrs. Dollahon, whose husband had died years before. It had a few canned goods, but they were caked in dust, and everything in the store looked like it had been on the shelves for at least ten years.

But the Andice post office was housed in Dollahon's, so every day there was a steady stream of people in and out of the store to pick up their mail. That meant that Mrs. Dollahon got to see people every day. They didn't buy many of her old, dusty canned goods, but they came to the store to get their mail, and, of course, they conversed with Mrs. Dollahon when they came.

There came the day, though, when the United States Postal Service decided to build a little post office building in Andice. It was a nice, brick building—much nicer than Dollahon's old store—and everyone in town started going to the new post office to get their mail. The traffic in and out of the store slowed to something less than a trickle. There were days when no one came at all. A few weeks after the new post office opened, Mrs. Dollahon quietly died in her sleep.

Several possible causes of death were mentioned. Some said she simply died of old age. Other said she had had a heart attack. Some surmised that she had had a stroke. No one seemed to know for certain why Mrs. Dollahon died. But there is another possibility, and it is the one I've always suspected. Mrs. Dollahon may have died because she no longer had a reason to get up in the morning. Once she lost her post office, she lost her purpose. She died because she lost her expectation, her hope.

I have no way of proving that, of course. But whether that was true for Mrs. Dollahon or not, I know that hope can die. I've seen it happen too many times. And when hope dies, life starts to wither. To put it bluntly, when hope dies, people die.

Hope-Killers

That is why it is essential that we understand how hope dies. There is no shortage of hope-killers in our world, and we have to be able to recognize them when they show up in our lives. Let me mention three common hope-killers:

First, *routine* can kill hope. We can be grateful that we have a routine to our lives, that there is a natural order of things, and that life is at least somewhat predictable. No one really wants to live in a topsy-turvy land where everything is unpredictable. We need to know that night follows day and that the seasons come and go with regular consistency. (Sherry used to have a shirt that said, "I love to watch the seasons change: football, basketball, baseball..."). I know that I am very much a creature of habit who likes routine and tradition.

But I also know that too much routine can kill expectancy. We can easily end up where the Teacher in Ecclesiastes ended up: so tired of the same thing day after day that life looks pointless. He concluded that there was nothing new under the sun and wondered if there was anything anywhere that could shake him out of his lethargy.

Compare that to Simeon's attitude: constantly expecting the Messiah to come soon. Even the daily routine in the temple was probably transformed into something exciting because he had something (or Someone) to look forward to.

One of the trickiest tightropes we all have to walk in life is enjoying and appreciating our routine without letting it kill our hope.

Second, *people* can kill hope. It's sad to acknowledge it, but it's true: some people are experts at killing hope in others. In his book *Restoring Your Spiritual Passion* (Nashville TN: Nelson, 1986), Gordon MacDonald discusses the five kinds of people in our lives:

- VRP: The Very Resourceful People who ignite our passion.
- VIP: The Very Important People who share our passion.
- VTP: The Very Trainable People who catch our passion.
- VNP: The Very Nice People who enjoy our passion.
- VDP: The Very Draining People who sap our passion.

Most of us have experienced those five kinds of people. At one end of the spectrum, some people ignite our passion and fill us with hope. At the other end of the spectrum, some people sap our passion and kill our hope.

And lest we consider ourselves only as victims of hope-killers, let's use that list to remind ourselves that we can be perpetrators of hope-killing, too. Do we unintentionally sap people's passion and destroy their hope? Or do we ignite their passion and increase their hope?

Another challenge we all have is living in the real world, where there are all kinds of people, without letting the VDPs completely kill our hope.

Third, *rigid expectations* can kill hope. That's what happened to many Jews in the first century. They had very rigid expectations regarding the coming Messiah, so they didn't recognize Jesus when he came. They just knew the Messiah would be a military ruler who would lead Israel back to a place of world prominence and power. Certainly, he would not be a baby in a bed of straw. Certainly, he would not be crucified on a cross. Most people in the first century didn't recognize Jesus for who he was because he didn't meet their messianic expectations. Let's give old Simeon his due. He was open to this baby, open to however God chose to reveal himself to the world.

Most of us have rigid expectations for how our lives are supposed to unfold. We have our future mapped out: marriage, children, finances, career, health, and all of the other components of a "successful" life. It's all clearly diagrammed in our minds. This is the way life and success will look for us.

When our life doesn't unfold the way we had it planned, though, it's easy to give up hope. We assume that since our reality hasn't matched the map in our minds, we must have failed. But if we will just be open to the possibility of a future we hadn't planned or anticipated, God can take the tattered remnants of our lives and create joy, love, and usefulness. God's Plan B can even turn out to be better than our Plan A.

A third challenge we all have to face is setting life goals without letting them become so rigid that they kill our hope if we don't reach them.

The Hope of Plan B

Christmas always reminds us that God doesn't do things the predictable way. No one would have concocted or predicted this story. Only a very unconventional Deity would have chosen to save the world through a baby born in a borrowed stable who grew up to be an outcast crucified on a Roman cross. But God did choose that method to redeem the world, and, if nothing else, the Christmas story ought to fill us with hope—especially if our Plan A has collapsed.

If we're one of those people convinced that marriage has to be this way, and success has to look like this, and the kids have to turn out like this, and none of those things has turned out the way we had planned, then we need the Christmas story. And we need to hear old Simeon singing his song of hope. We need that song because it comes from someone who never gave up hope, someone who woke up every morning looking for the Messiah.

Then, touched by Simeon's capacity to live on tiptoe, we can try living that way ourselves. We can quit trying so hard to be successful and lean into the sovereignty of God. We can let God work and trust that the collapse of our plan might just be the beginning of something better for us.

Conclusion

Throughout this study, we have been listening to people singing:

- The prophet in Isaiah sang about the servant who felt weary and used up but was called by God anyway.
- Mary sang about the wonder of God choosing someone like her.
- Zechariah sang about the birth of his child and the other Child who would be a light to anyone sitting in the darkness.
- The angels sang their song of joy, reminding us that our good news is even better than we know.
- Simeon sang because his hope had been realized and his dream of seeing the promised one had come true.

We've been listening to these people singing with one fervent hope: that their songs might be so contagious that we will start singing, too. We know that the best thing we can offer the world is not our doctrine, advice, wisdom, condemnation, or money. The best thing we can offer the world is our song.

Good and gracious God, as we have listened to Simeon sing today, we realize what a wonderful thing hope is. Help us never run out of hope. Keep us living on tiptoe so that we will live to the end of our days. In the spirit of Isaiah, Mary, Zechariah, the angels, and Simeon, keep us singing our song of joy. In the name and spirit of the promised one we pray, Amen.

Notes

Notes

www.ingramcontent.com/pod-product-compliance
Lightning Source LLC
Chambersburg PA
CBHW070552030426
42337CB00016B/2464